MW00943074

All The Reasons The Minnesota Golden Gophers Are Better Than The Wisconsin Badgers

All The Reasons The
Minnesota Golden Gophers
Are Better Than The
Wisconsin Badgers

A Comprehensive Look At All Of The Superior Qualities Of The Univesrity Of Minnesota Compared To The University Of Wisconsin

Jeff Slutsky

© Copyright 2015 by Jeff Slutsky.

All rights reserved. This book may not be reproduced, in whole or part, in any form or by an means electronic or mechanical, including photocopy, recording or by any information storage and retrieval system now known or hereafter invented, without written permission from the author.

All The Reasons The Minnesota Golden Gophers
Are Better Than The Wisconsin Badgers

To order this book on line: https://www.alltheresasons.net

ISBN-13: 978-1505657227
ISBN-10: 1505657229

Dedication

This book is dedicated to the fans of The University of Wisconsin .

Also available by By Jeff Slutsky

All The Reasons LSU Tigers Are Better Than The Alabama Crimson Tide

All The Reasons Michigan Is Better Than Ohio State

All The Reasons The Army Black Knights Are Better Than The Navy Midshipment

All The Reasons To Love Obamacare

All The Reasons I Love Accounting

Some More Serious Books By Jeff Slutsky

More Smart Marketing
Smart Selling
From The Big Screen to the Real World
Totastmaster's Guide To Successful Speaking
Street Fighter Marketing Solutions
No B.S. Grassroots Marketing

To order books - https://www.allthereasons.net

THIS PAGE IS BLANK DUE TO LACK OF REASONS

THIS PAGE IS BLANK DUE TO LACK OF REASONS

THIS PAGE IS BLANK DUE TO LACK OF REASONS

THIS PAGE IS BLANK DUE TO LACK OF REASONS

THIS PAGE IS BLANK DUE TO LACK OF REASONS

THIS PAGE IS BLANK DUE TO LACK OF REASONS

THIS PAGE IS BLANK DUE TO LACK OF REASONS

THIS PAGE IS BLANK DUE TO LACK OF REASONS

THIS PAGE IS BLANK DUE TO LACK OF REASONS

THIS PAGE IS BLANK DUE TO LACK OF REASONS

THIS PAGE IS BLANK DUE TO LACK OF REASONS

THIS PAGE IS BLANK DUE TO LACK OF REASONS

THIS PAGE IS BLANK DUE TO LACK OF REASONS

THIS PAGE IS BLANK DUE TO LACK OF REASONS

THIS PAGE IS BLANK DUE TO LACK OF REASONS

THIS PAGE IS BLANK DUE TO LACK OF REASONS

THIS PAGE IS BLANK DUE TO LACK OF REASONS

THIS PAGE IS BLANK DUE TO LACK OF REASONS

THIS PAGE IS BLANK DUE TO LACK OF REASONS

THIS PAGE IS BLANK DUE TO LACK OF REASONS

THIS PAGE IS BLANK DUE TO LACK OF REASONS

THIS PAGE IS BLANK DUE TO LACK OF REASONS

THIS PAGE IS BLANK DUE TO LACK OF REASONS

THIS PAGE IS BLANK DUE TO LACK OF REASONS

THIS PAGE IS BLANK DUE TO LACK OF REASONS

THIS PAGE IS BLANK DUE TO LACK OF REASONS

THIS PAGE IS BLANK DUE TO LACK OF REASONS

THIS PAGE IS BLANK DUE TO LACK OF REASONS

THIS PAGE IS BLANK DUE TO LACK OF REASONS

THIS PAGE IS BLANK DUE TO LACK OF REASONS

THIS PAGE IS BLANK DUE TO LACK OF REASONS

THIS PAGE IS BLANK DUE TO LACK OF REASONS

THIS PAGE IS BLANK DUE TO LACK OF REASONS

THIS PAGE IS BLANK DUE TO LACK OF REASONS

THIS PAGE IS BLANK DUE TO LACK OF REASONS

THIS PAGE IS BLANK DUE TO LACK OF REASONS

THIS PAGE IS BLANK DUE TO LACK OF REASONS

THIS PAGE IS BLANK DUE TO LACK OF REASONS

THIS PAGE IS BLANK DUE TO LACK OF REASONS

THIS PAGE IS BLANK DUE TO LACK OF REASONS

THIS PAGE IS BLANK DUE TO LACK OF REASONS

THIS PAGE IS BLANK DUE TO LACK OF REASONS

THIS PAGE IS BLANK DUE TO LACK OF REASONS

THIS PAGE IS BLANK DUE TO LACK OF REASONS

THIS PAGE IS BLANK DUE TO LACK OF REASONS

THIS PAGE IS BLANK DUE TO LACK OF REASONS

THIS PAGE IS BLANK DUE TO LACK OF REASONS

THIS PAGE IS BLANK DUE TO LACK OF REASONS

THIS PAGE IS BLANK DUE TO LACK OF REASONS

THIS PAGE IS BLANK DUE TO LACK OF REASONS

THIS PAGE IS BLANK DUE TO LACK OF REASONS

THIS PAGE IS BLANK DUE TO LACK OF REASONS

THIS PAGE IS BLANK DUE TO LACK OF REASONS

THIS PAGE IS BLANK DUE TO LACK OF REASONS

THIS PAGE IS BLANK DUE TO LACK OF REASONS

THIS PAGE IS BLANK DUE TO LACK OF REASONS

THIS PAGE IS BLANK DUE TO LACK OF REASONS

THIS PAGE IS BLANK DUE TO LACK OF REASONS

THIS PAGE IS BLANK DUE TO LACK OF REASONS

THIS PAGE IS BLANK DUE TO LACK OF REASONS

THIS PAGE IS BLANK DUE TO LACK OF REASONS

THIS PAGE IS BLANK DUE TO LACK OF REASONS

THIS PAGE IS BLANK DUE TO LACK OF REASONS

THIS PAGE IS BLANK DUE TO LACK OF REASONS

THIS PAGE IS BLANK DUE TO LACK OF REASONS

THIS PAGE IS BLANK DUE TO LACK OF REASONS

THIS PAGE IS BLANK DUE TO LACK OF REASONS

THIS PAGE IS BLANK DUE TO LACK OF REASONS

THIS PAGE IS BLANK DUE TO LACK OF REASONS

THIS PAGE IS BLANK DUE TO LACK OF REASONS

THIS PAGE IS BLANK DUE TO LACK OF REASONS

THIS PAGE IS BLANK DUE TO LACK OF REASONS

THIS PAGE IS BLANK DUE TO LACK OF REASONS

THIS PAGE IS BLANK DUE TO LACK OF REASONS

THIS PAGE IS BLANK DUE TO LACK OF REASONS

THIS PAGE IS BLANK DUE TO LACK OF REASONS

THIS PAGE IS BLANK DUE TO LACK OF REASONS

THIS PAGE IS BLANK DUE TO LACK OF REASONS

THIS PAGE IS BLANK DUE TO LACK OF REASONS

THIS PAGE IS BLANK DUE TO LACK OF REASONS

THIS PAGE IS BLANK DUE TO LACK OF REASONS

THIS PAGE IS BLANK DUE TO LACK OF REASONS

THIS PAGE IS BLANK DUE TO LACK OF REASONS

THIS PAGE IS BLANK DUE TO LACK OF REASONS

THIS PAGE IS BLANK DUE TO LACK OF REASONS

THIS PAGE IS BLANK DUE TO LACK OF REASONS

THIS PAGE IS BLANK DUE
TO LACK OF REASONS

THIS PAGE IS BLANK DUE TO LACK OF REASONS

THIS PAGE IS BLANK DUE TO LACK OF REASONS

THIS PAGE IS BLANK DUE TO LACK OF REASONS

THIS PAGE IS BLANK DUE TO LACK OF REASONS

THIS PAGE IS BLANK DUE TO LACK OF REASONS

THIS PAGE IS BLANK DUE TO LACK OF REASONS

THIS PAGE IS BLANK DUE TO LACK OF REASONS

THIS PAGE IS BLANK DUE TO LACK OF REASONS

THIS PAGE IS BLANK DUE TO LACK OF REASONS

THIS PAGE IS BLANK DUE TO LACK OF REASONS

THIS PAGE IS BLANK DUE
TO LACK OF REASONS

THIS PAGE IS BLANK DUE TO LACK OF REASONS

THIS PAGE IS BLANK DUE TO LACK OF REASONS

THIS PAGE IS BLANK DUE TO LACK OF REASONS

THIS PAGE IS BLANK DUE TO LACK OF REASONS

THIS PAGE IS BLANK DUE TO LACK OF REASONS

THIS PAGE IS BLANK DUE TO LACK OF REASONS

THIS PAGE IS BLANK DUE TO LACK OF REASONS

THIS PAGE IS BLANK DUE TO LACK OF REASONS

THIS PAGE IS BLANK DUE TO LACK OF REASONS

THIS PAGE IS BLANK DUE TO LACK OF REASONS

THIS PAGE IS BLANK DUE TO LACK OF REASONS

THIS PAGE IS BLANK DUE TO LACK OF REASONS

THIS PAGE IS BLANK DUE TO LACK OF REASONS

THIS PAGE IS BLANK DUE TO LACK OF REASONS

THIS PAGE IS BLANK DUE TO LACK OF REASONS

THIS PAGE IS BLANK DUE TO LACK OF REASONS

THIS PAGE IS BLANK DUE TO LACK OF REASONS

THIS PAGE IS BLANK DUE TO LACK OF REASONS

THIS PAGE IS BLANK DUE TO LACK OF REASONS

THIS PAGE IS BLANK DUE TO LACK OF REASONS

THIS PAGE IS BLANK DUE TO LACK OF REASONS

THIS PAGE IS BLANK DUE TO LACK OF REASONS

THIS PAGE IS BLANK DUE TO LACK OF REASONS

THIS PAGE IS BLANK DUE TO LACK OF REASONS

THIS PAGE IS BLANK DUE TO LACK OF REASONS

THIS PAGE IS BLANK DUE TO LACK OF REASONS

THIS PAGE IS BLANK DUE TO LACK OF REASONS

THIS PAGE IS BLANK DUE TO LACK OF REASONS

FROM THE CO-AUTHOR

Getting More From Your People Has Never Been More Fun! With Jeff Slutsky's Hilarious Motivational Speech

"This is the fourth time we've worked with Jeff and he was better than ever! Very funny, great content, engaging and easy to work with."

-- Michael Jeffreys, CEO, Seminars on Demand

Give Your Success A Shot In The Arm with Slutsky's

INFLUENCE BOOSTER ®

Jeff Slutsky's new, maximum strength motivational speech, is infused with all-natural street-savvy ideas and hilarious anecdotes that empowers your people to succeed during these hyper stressful times. Let Slutsky immunize your attendees from results-deficiency and anemic performance. While laughter may be the best medicine, today's environment demands that humor be enhanced with equal parts: content, audience interaction and practical, proven ideas for those who suffer from mild to moderate apathy. That's why the new and improved, INFLUENCE BOOSTER keynote speech, is now available without a prescription and ready to be administered at your meeting or convention. Ask your meeting planner if Slutsky's INFLUENCE BOOSTER is right for you. Use only as directed.

Call or Email Today for Fees and Availabilities

Nancy Lauterbach • O:480.366.4040 • C:913.488.6480 • nancy@redprops.com

Bill Lauterbach • office: 480.366.4040 • cell: 913.706.0241 • bill@redprops.com

Kathy Popplewell Morris • office: (425) 221-1728 • kathy@redprops.com

To order more copies of this book on line:

https://www.alltheresons.net

Also Available:

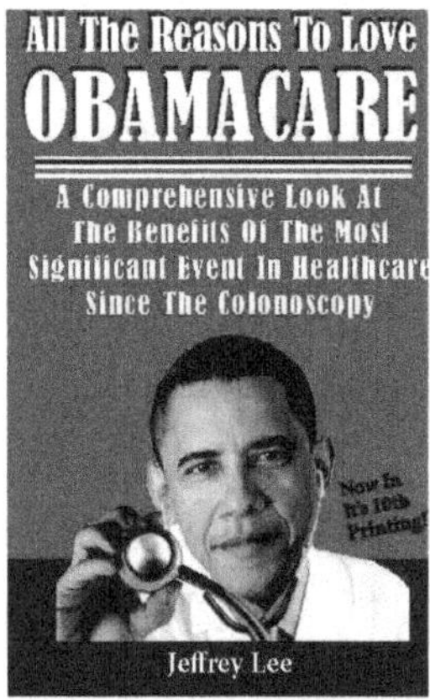

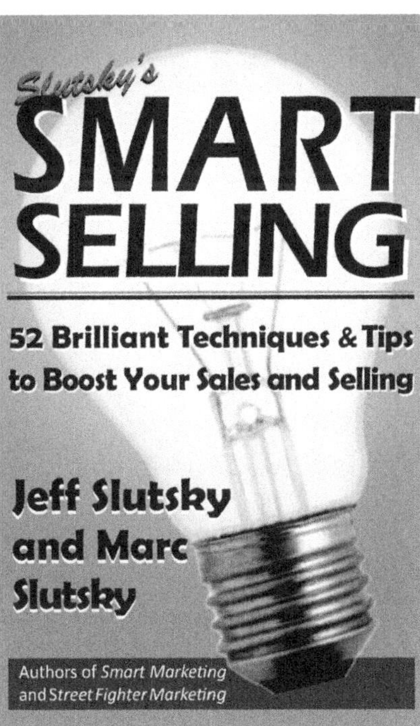

To order *More Smart Marketing:*

www.createspace.com/4403184

To order *Smart Selling:*

www.createspace.com/4411673

Made in the USA
Middletown, DE
10 November 2019